TWO
HORSEMEN

To Rebecca

'BIYI BANDELE-THOMAS

TWO
HORSEMEN

AMBER LANE PRESS

All rights whatsoever in this play are strictly reserved and application for performance, etc. must be made before rehearsals begin to:

MBA Literary Agents Ltd
45 Fitzroy Street
London W1P 5HR

No performance may be given unless a licence has been obtained.

First published in 1994 by
Amber Lane Press Ltd,
Cheorl House, Church Street,
Charlbury, Oxford OX7 3PR
Telephone: 0608 810024

Printed in Great Britain by
Bocardo Press Ltd, Didcot, Oxon.

ISBN 1 872868 12 6

TWO HORSEMEN was first presented at the Gate Theatre on 27 July 1994 as part of the London New Play Festival. The cast was as follows:

BANZA .... Leo Wringer
LAGBAJA .... Colin McFarlane

Director: Roxana Silbert
Assistant Director: Sian Edwards
Designer: Naomi Wilkinson

Acknowledgements

To Alan Ayckbourn, Burt Caesar, Eddie Nestor,
Jude Akuwudike and a host of others
— too many to list here —
whose help and generosity took this play,
in an earlier draft, to the
National Student Drama Festival, Scarborough, in 1990.

And thanks once again to Clive and Pat Wolfe,
without whom ...

Characters

BANZA

LAGBAJA

Setting

A room somewhere: a dirty, scrap-filled room whose only claim to fame is a broken-down bed, a battered coffee-table and two cane chairs that have certainly seen kinder days. A kerosene stove. Pots and plates. A hurricane lamp against the wall. Beside this, a dead old clock. Shirts, trousers, books and newspapers flung carelessly everywhere.

A coin-operated telephone is situated by the door.

ACT ONE: *Rain*

*The lights come up on the room. It is early
evening. BANZA and LAGBAJA are sitting stone-
faced, looking intently at each other, as if
studying specimens in a laboratory glass case.*

BANZA   It rained yesterday, did you know that?

LAGBAJA   Really. I didn't know that.

BANZA   You didn't know that it rained yesterday?

LAGBAJA   I must've been too busy at my sweeping to
have noticed.

BANZA   You sweep?

LAGBAJA   Streets, sure, that's my job. Always been my
job. Twenty, maybe thirty years now. A family trade actually.

BANZA   Cleaning streets?

LAGBAJA   Handed over from one generation to the
next.

BANZA   Well, my friend, it did rain yesterday.

LAGBAJA   Was the ground wet?

BANZA   Cats and dogs. But mostly water. You
should've seen it. Mud everywhere. In the
streets, under the bridge, at the beer-
parlour, the church ...

LAGBAJA   Oh no! Not there as well. Please don't you
ever say that again, not even in jest — mud
in the beer-parlour!

BANZA   Well, it happened, and that's it, whether you like it or not.

LAGBAJA   You were there? You saw it?

BANZA   I was there, I saw it. Mud in the beer-parlour. Never seen the like of it in all my life. This disgusting, utterly disgusting carpet of mud in the beer-parlour. Of all places, for christsake. I almost threw up.

LAGBAJA   Ah, that explains it then.

BANZA   What?

LAGBAJA   The beer, last night. Tasted like mud. I could've sworn it. I almost puked.

BANZA   Well, for one thing, it wasn't like you to be so sad after such a fine day at the beer-parlour. And when you burst into that fit of drunken laughter — that was when I said to myself, I said to myself, something must be wrong with Mensa.

LAGBAJA   And something was wrong with me, old friend. My beer tasted like mud. That's what was wrong, like mud, my friend!

BANZA   I was about getting around to asking you what was the matter — being the good friend that I happen to be ...

LAGBAJA   ... and realising too, I suppose, that a friend in need ...

BANZA   ... is a pain in the neck. Moreover, that's when you farted. And everyone ran for cover.

LAGBAJA   Me, fart? [*indignantly*] I'll have you know,
            sir, that I take exception to such blatant
            defamation of my character, such cold-
            blooded campaign of calamity —

BANZA   Calumny.

LAGBAJA   — that too ... on my person.

BANZA   Hey, hey. Don't get worked up over nothing.
            You farted, and that's all. No big deal. I used
            to be quite — prolific myself. At farting. It
            was my speciality in primary school ... but,
            come to think of it, it wasn't really my fault.
            My old man's idea of a balanced diet, you
            see, was ...

LAGBAJA)   [*together*] ... mashed beans for breakfast,
BANZA)   bean-cake and garri for lunch, and mashed
            beans again for supper.

BANZA   Balanced, my foot, you might say. But you
            should've seen me in those days. Round like
            a ball. They used to call me Michelin — and
            I'd wave — and then break wind. I was so
            good at it no one ever knew I was the one.

            [*He moves around as he speaks.*]

            But one day, I pushed my luck too far. It was
            during an arithmetic lesson, I remember.
            The mistress said, "Class, what are two plus
            two?" And we answered —

LAGBAJA   "Two plus two are five."

            [*Pause.*]

BANZA   Erm, yes. And she was so pleased with us, with our precocious intellect, our superb arithmetic, and was, in fact, heaping praise on us when — I broke wind. Booooon! A cross between a rotten egg and a decomposing dead body. The teacher — Mississ Shorum we used to call her on account she was married to this man called Mr Aaron, which in our barely weaned mouths came out simply as "Shorum" — came to a dead halt in front of the class. [*mimics*] "Wish of you messed?" she asked slowly, casting her stern, furious eyes on our frightened little faces. "I said, who messed? *Ta lo so?*" * No one said a word. I dared not breathe. I was trembling in my seat. "Ah, so you're not going to confess, abi. Well, I am going to find the culprit today-today, do you hear me, I am going to cash that bad-egg today-today, that lack-of-home-training shild who was not fearing to come and mess inside class amongst a civilized society. I am going to cash him or her today-today. Oya, all of you, useless shildren, stand up." So we all got to our feet. And — you won't believe this — what she did next — she embarked on a sniffing exercise: she would drag a child up from his seat, raise his arms close to her nose and sniff. Satisfied you weren't her man she'd put you back on your seat and go on to

---

* YORUBA: Who farted?

the next suspect. One by one she went round the class, sniffing one arse after the other, but it seemed her culprit would never be caught. That is, until she came to yours truly. I'd been trembling before she came to my desk, but the moment she came, the trembling stopped. The same routine: she pulled me by the trouser, lifted me up to her nose-level and sniffed. Luckily for me, the stench of the "blast" had been blown away by the wind long before she came to me, so I was quite confident I was going to pass the scrutiny. But I made this assumption without including my buttocks — and it turned out to be a terrible oversight. I was right up there in the air, confidently defying gravity courtesy of Mississ Shorum, happily bearing the supreme humiliation of having my arse sniffed at, when I heard this terrible, utterly horrible sound come out from — none other than — my arse! It was like the sound of a car with a bad silencer. You should've seen Mississ Shorum that morning.

LAGBAJA   What did she do to you?

BANZA   Do? For the next five minutes she wasn't in any position to do anything. Remember she was so close to the site of the explosion. She was on sick leave a whole week. After that she wouldn't have me in her class.

LAGBAJA   Really! Wouldn't have you in her class! The very idea! As if she owned the school! Didn't you tell your old man? And didn't he come marching indignantly to school with you the next day?

BANZA   No, he didn't.

LAGBAJA   But he should have!

BANZA   Well, he didn't.

LAGBAJA   But, why didn't he?

BANZA   He was Mr Shorum.

LAGBAJA   You mean ... [*the penny drops*] Mississ Shorum's husband?

BANZA   The one and only.

LAGBAJA   And Mississ Shorum — she was your mother?

BANZA   None other.

LAGBAJA   And you farted in her mouth? Your mother's mouth?

BANZA   She deserved it. Had it coming. Teach her to go sniffing people's arses, that's what I thought.

LAGBAJA   What a right bastard you were.

BANZA   Just her word, bastard. That's what she called me.

LAGBAJA   She did? I would too.

BANZA   And I said, "Well, if you say so mother, I'll take your word for it."

LAGBAJA   My God. You make me sick. That's no way to treat your mother.

BANZA   She asked for it.

LAGBAJA   Naughty, naughty, naughty boy.

BANZA   Come to think of it, there never was a time when I was on good terms with her.

LAGBAJA   Never? Oh come on — not even when you were but a fetish inside her?

BANZA   A what?

LAGBAJA   You know, before you were born?

BANZA   A foetus. No, not even then. She was given to drinking, you see. Guinness, nothing but Guinness. But I hated bitter tasting drinks. So anytime she took Guinness, I'd kick her in the stomach.

LAGBAJA   I'm sure you don't expect me to believe that fairy-tale?

BANZA   No, I don't.

LAGBAJA   Funnily enough, I do. It's too unbelievable to be a lie.

BANZA   For your information, it's a lie.

[*The phone begins to ring.*]

I cooked the whole thing up.

LAGBAJA   The more reason that I should believe it.

[*They listen to the phone without making any effort to attend to it. It stops.*]

It rained yesterday, did you know that?

BANZA   Really. I didn't know that.

LAGBAJA   You didn't know that it rained yesterday?

BANZA   I must've been too busy at my sweeping to have noticed.

LAGBAJA   You sweep — ?

  BANZA   Streets, yes, that's my job. Always been my job. Twenty, maybe, thirty years now. A family trade actually.

LAGBAJA   Cleaning streets?

  BANZA   Handed over from one generation to the next.

LAGBAJA   Well, my friend, it did rain yesterday. Cats and dogs and what have you.

  BANZA   Was the ground wet?

LAGBAJA   Everywhere.

  BANZA   Did folks bring out their umbrellas?

LAGBAJA   Of all colours of the rainbow.

  BANZA   And those without umbrellas?

LAGBAJA   Raincoats. Mackintoshes.

  BANZA   And those without raincoats, mackintoshes?

LAGBAJA   Got beaten by the rain, of course.

  BANZA   And why should some have umbrellas and others none?

LAGBAJA   I'd like you to tell me. It's always been like that.

  BANZA   Always?

LAGBAJA   Always.

              [*Pause.*]

          Who cares anyway? I'm not God. That's God's business. To give folks umbrellas.

  BANZA   I met him yesterday, on the bus.

[*The phone rings. It ceases on the second ring as* BANZA *makes as if to get it.*]

Did I tell you?

LAGBAJA   Who?

BANZA   God. Sat right next to him on the bus yesterday.

LAGBAJA   [*enthralled*] You did? You — actually met God? Oh my God! How'd he look like?

BANZA   Have you ever seen any of those sleazy Kung Fu films? [*voice change*] Ding dong ding! You killed my papa when I was a kid, now I'm gonna kill you...

[*He assumes a Kung Fu posture, arms spread as if about to fly. He feigns at* LAGBAJA, *who has also assumed a similar posture.*]

Over the rivers! Wham! Across the mountains! Ggrramm! Into the paddy-fields! Over the tree-tops! Into the temple!

[*They battle each other using every detachable object in the room as weapons.* BANZA *deals* LAGBAJA *a "lethal" blow.*]

That's how he looked. God. Like a character straight out of those meaningless gory tales. In fact, to be precise, he looked ... like a Chinese mandarin. Long, grey beard, a garrotte in his hand. As weird as they come. And his breath stank of whisky. One swig too many, I guess. Can't grudge him that, though, not with what his world has turned into. Enough to make anyone hit the bottle. He was singing too. [*sings*] "Sometimes I feel like a motherless child ..."

LAGBAJA   Are you, are you sure that wasn't the devil you met?

BANZA   No, it wasn't. Couldn't have been, it was God. I knew it was him. What's more, he was talking dirty to the girl in the front seat.

LAGBAJA   God? The Almighty? Talking dirty? No, Mensa. A joke is a joke. I'm sorry, that couldn't have been God.

BANZA   Well, it was. He told me so himself.

LAGBAJA   Oh, he did?

BANZA   Yes, I asked him and he said to me, "Yes my son, I am God." And he lay a hand on my forehead and blessed me.

LAGBAJA   [*excited*] He blessed you? God actually blessed you?

BANZA   [*proudly*] Yes sir, he did. Placed his hand on me like this and said in his vibrant sonorous voice, "Cursed be the day you were born, my son."

LAGBAJA   And I suppose you said "Amen".

BANZA   Of course I did. What do you take me for? A dunce?

          [*He fishes out a tin of cheap untipped cigarettes from the inner pocket of his coat.*]

You will bore a man to death, Mensa.

[*He throws a cigarette to* LAGBAJA, *holds one himself and returns the tin very carefully to his pocket.*]

Every day you just sit there and yap. Does nothing ever happen in your life?

LAGBAJA   Nothing. Nor in yours, come to think of it.

BANZA   Every day we just sit here and yap away our lives.

LAGBAJA   Our lives? I thought I once heard you say we had none.

BANZA   Well, in all honesty, do we? Our lives rolled to a stand-still a long time ago. Like that thing over there on the wall. Now we're only waiting for the rust to set in.

LAGBAJA   For the worms to fall onto the carrion?

BANZA   For the crumbling wall to cave in and bash in the wandering head of the wayfarer.

LAGBAJA   Do you realise that I hate your guts? Every time I'm with you, I'm infected by this senseless melancholy of yours. Can't you ever see anything good in anything?

BANZA   You're growing old gracefully. You are becoming senile.

[*Pause.*]

Do you want to hear a story?

LAGBAJA   Not another of those crackpot stories of yours, I hope.

[*He sniffs his cigarette appreciatively.*]

Having nothing against the good things of life — I'll say shoot on. I have nothing against — dating a fine woman — or hearing a good story. They go together, have you noticed that?   Women and stories.   Tall stories. And that, by the way, is the story of my life.

BANZA   Mine too. Plenty of stories but no women.

LAGBAJA   None at all?

BANZA   Not even one.

LAGBAJA   Not even your mother?

BANZA   Do I look like someone who had a mother?

LAGBAJA   No. You don't.

BANZA   I never knew my mother.

LAGBAJA   Oh God, not another sob story. Whatever happened to her?

BANZA   [*griefstricken*] She died in an accident.

LAGBAJA   An accident?

BANZA   A bicycle accident.

LAGBAJA   Oh my God. Was she riding one and got hit by a car or something?

BANZA   No. She was walking to the market and got hit by a bicycle.

LAGBAJA   And died?

BANZA   No, of course not! She wasn't killed by the bicycle. It was the cyclist did her in. [*demonstrates a physical assault*] She fell into a coma and never woke up.

[*Pause.*]

It was a deadly bicycle accident.

LAGBAJA   What about the Shorums? I thought you mentioned them ...

BANZA   Yes, I did. The Shorums. Nice couple. Bless their souls.

LAGBAJA   As your parents.

BANZA   No, I didn't.

LAGBAJA   Yes, you did.

BANZA   No, I didn't.

LAGBAJA   But you did. Be man enough to admit it. You did!

BANZA   Okay, okay, slip of the tongue. I had no parents. Never knew my mother. She walked out on my old man just before I was born. So he had to bring me up all on his own.

[*Pause.*]

Before he too died shortly afterwards.

LAGBAJA   [*feelingly*] Poor fellow.

BANZA   Yeah, that's what I am. A poor fellow.

LAGBAJA   Your father, not you, idiot.

BANZA   And he was too, an absolute nonentity. Woke up one day after watching a match on TV and decided he wanted to be a footballer. He was sixty then. And some. Someone mistook him for the football and kicked him into the net. That's how come I ended up in an orphanage.

LAGBAJA   I don't like it at all. The way you talk about your father.

BANZA   Oh, well, I'm sorry.

LAGBAJA   [*suddenly angry*] Why did you do that?

BANZA   Do what?

LAGBAJA   Why did you say "Oh"?

BANZA   Why shouldn't I?

LAGBAJA   Because it gets me down. Every time I hear someone say "Oh" I get the blues. It reminds me of the one woman I've ever had in all my life. She was always saying "Oh".

BANZA   Oh, what?

LAGBAJA   There you go again.

BANZA   I'm sorry. But what happened to her? She leave you? Or you left her?

LAGBAJA   Twenty years, Mensa, for twenty years we were married, this woman and I, and never had a baby.

BANZA   What was the matter with you: a faulty kick starter? Couldn't you get it up?

[LAGBAJA *leans over and whispers into* BANZA's *ear.*]

[*incredulous*] She wouldn't let you! And she was your wife! For twenty years! I hope you're misquoting yourself. Why didn't you just call it quits with her?

LAGBAJA   [*sheepishly*] Now that you say it ...

BANZA   ... it never occurred to you?

LAGBAJA   Never. But not to worry. I got her in the
           end.

BANZA   [*eagerly*] You did? You did?

LAGBAJA   You bet I did. Would you believe that for
           those twenty years, for those three hundred
           and forty months she never let me near her,
           she was only pretending, and was actually
           dying for me!

           [BANZA *regards him sceptically.*]

           One day —

           [*He inserts the cigarette between his lips.*]

           She came in from the market — [*He stops.*]

BANZA   She came in from the market ... ?

LAGBAJA   She made me a nice meal, the nicest in fact
           that I'd had in years, and knowing her man's
           "fluid" tastes, topped it all with a well im-
           prisoned beer.

BANZA   That's how I like my beer. Well imprisoned.
           You must've been swooning by then, I know.

LAGBAJA   Well, I wasn't. I was as calm and cool as any
           man whose wife decides to give him a
           scrumpy lunch and a ...

BANZA   ... scrummy ...

LAGBAJA   ... that's what I said. A scrumpy lunch for a
           treat and a mercilessly chilled beer to wit.
           No less. Anyway, after all this, she brought
           out from her bag this strange little thing that
           looked like a balloon and told me to wear it
           on my what's-its-name.

BANZA   Your what's-its-name?

LAGBAJA   Yes, my what's-its-name.

BANZA   What's your what's-its-name?

LAGBAJA   My what's-its-name.

BANZA   Your what's-its-name is your what's-its-name?

LAGBAJA   Precisely.

BANZA   Very well, go on.

LAGBAJA   She brought out this thing that looked like a balloon and told me to wear it on my what's-its-name.

BANZA   What was that thing that looked like a balloon?

LAGBAJA) [*together*] Something that looked like a
BANZA)   balloon.

BANZA   Yes. But what was it?

LAGBAJA   That's it. Something that looked like a balloon.

BANZA   In other words, this thing that looked like a balloon was something that looked like a balloon.

          [*He fishes out the tin of cigarettes. He takes back the cigarette from* LAGBAJA *and returns it, with his own, to the tin. He returns the tin to his pocket.*]

LAGBAJA   Precisely.

BANZA   Very well, go on.

LAGBAJA   I wore this thing that looked like a balloon

on my what's-its-name, then we got down to business.

[*Pause.*]

BANZA   What does that mean: "down to business"?

LAGBAJA   That means we made love, idiot.

BANZA   You made love? [*giggles*] To your wife for the first time in twenty years? [*giggles again*] And I suppose that thing that looked like a balloon was a condom?

LAGBAJA   What?

BANZA   A condom. A raincoat. A parachute. Was it a condom or wasn't it?

LAGBAJA   Is that what they call it? A hell lot of use it was, the useless thing. Fell inside right in the middle of the job!

BANZA   [*horrified*] Oh, God! Inside?

LAGBAJA   [*sighs at the memory*] Yes. Right inside. And ... [*brightens*] ... that's how she became a mother. You should have seen her — so furious. Called me names too. And then the baby came into the world. Wearing a cap.

BANZA   The baby was born with a cap on its head?

LAGBAJA   That's what I said.

BANZA   Could the cap have been the ... ?

LAGBAJA   The very same.

BANZA   ... that fell inside?

LAGBAJA   The very same.

[*Pause.*]

BANZA　　You lucky devil! And where are they now, your wife and kid?

LAGBAJA　I don't know.

BANZA　　You bastard! You walked out on her? You're an absentee father?

LAGBAJA　She walked out on me.

BANZA　　She walked out on you?

LAGBAJA　Yes.

BANZA　　May I know the reason?

LAGBAJA　I called out a name while we were ... you know, making love.

BANZA　　And it wasn't her name?

LAGBAJA　It wasn't her name.

BANZA　　So she walked out on you. Rightly too. Twenty years, man! Twenty years of her life, that's what you threw down the drain. My God! Some bastard you are, cheating on someone who's given twenty years of her life to you!

LAGBAJA　[*miserably*] I wasn't cheating on her.

BANZA　　Oh no, just having a bit of fun on the side. Whose name then did you call out in the heat of passion — yours?

LAGBAJA　As a matter of fact, yes. We were making love and I called out my name.

BANZA　　Sometimes in this life, Mensa, self-love is worse than cheating on your wife.

　　　　　[*Pause.*]

LAGBAJA My name is not Mensa.

[*Pause.*]

Do you want to know how I met her?

BANZA Met who?

LAGBAJA My wife. Who else? Your asthmatic father?

BANZA Point of correction. It wasn't asthma my father had. All he ever had in all his life was an ingrowing tooth that developed into tuberculosis.

LAGBAJA An ingrowing tooth that developed into tuberculosis?

BANZA Yes.

[*Pause.*]

LAGBAJA I met her at school.

BANZA Your wife?

LAGBAJA My wife.

BANZA [*bored*] I don't want to hear your story.

LAGBAJA I'll always remember that day. It was a bitterly cold morning. It was so hot that people were being felled at random by sunstroke. It was evening. She was studying in an empty classroom when I first saw her. I tried to catch her attention. She wouldn't even spare me a look before she packed her books, sprang up and headed for another class, a crowded one this time. And ...

BANZA You followed her.

LAGBAJA   Yes... I followed her. After a long while she gave me a withering look and stood up again and headed this time for the library, which was crowded as usual. I whispered fiercely to her: "I love you. I'm not going to let you rest until you acknowledge that love." She begged me to leave her alone but I wouldn't budge. Then suddenly, in a loud voice, she said: "Leave me alone! Stop disturbing me!" All eyes in the library were turned on us. I froze. Petrified. Wishing the ground would open up — and swallow her. Then I had a brainstorm. A brainstorm! I cleared my throat and said in a voice as loud as hers: "I will not leave you alone! I will not stop disturbing you until you accept Jesus Christ as your Lord and Saviour!"

BANZA   And that was how you ended up getting hitched?

LAGBAJA   We started quarrelling almost immediately.

BANZA   Why?

LAGBAJA   I was several hours late for the wedding. Clean forgot that it was my wedding.

          [*Pause.*]

          Got a cigarette to spare?

          [BANZA *brings out the tin and gives him a cigarette.*]

          For three days I've been looking for a cigarette to smoke.

[*He sniffs approvingly at the cigarette then returns it wordlessly to* BANZA.]

BANZA   For three days I've been coming out every night around this time to look at the night in all its vast meaninglessness.

[LAGBAJA *looks lengthily at an imaginary wristwatch.*]

LAGBAJA Is it night already?

BANZA   Do you have to be told?

LAGBAJA But I can still see the sun outside.

BANZA   Makes no difference one way or another.

LAGBAJA But, but if the sun is still out, does it not follow that it's still day?

BANZA   You stretch my patience. You and fools like you who go about staggering in this vast void of darkness and yet will talk about seeing the sun and the moon and the stars and all sorts of things! It's always night, do you hear that? Always one dark, starless night with the dead walking abroad and your hair standing on end, and your teeth clattering from fright, do you hear that? The sun and the moon and the stars are only illusions. They've never been there. Only the night exists, real, foreboding, with all those mega-headed monsters playing football with human skulls. Every other thing — sun, moon, star — is swallowed whole in the anger of the night.

LAGBAJA Pretty bleak, wouldn't you say? Yet from day to day the world continues to thrive.

BANZA   One day, I tell you, we'll all wake up and be covered by a sudden sweat.

LAGBAJA Hey, can't you look on the bright side for once? Don't you ever project into the future?

BANZA   Into the future? No, thanks. I'm not finished with the present yet. As to the future: when I get to that bridge ...

LAGBAJA ... you'll step on the broken planks and fall down the river, yes thank you. Ever heard of being optimistic?

BANZA   At the funeral of my best friend.

LAGBAJA I thought I was your best friend.

BANZA   Who said you weren't?

[*Pause.*]

It rained yesterday, did you know that?

LAGBAJA It's been so many years since it rained.

BANZA   Everywhere was wet.

LAGBAJA I was a kid when last it rained.

BANZA   The parched farmlands were flooded, trees bearing fruit uprooted, animals drowned, houses swept away.

LAGBAJA Is that what life is all about? Droughts and floods and nothing else?

BANZA   People were killed too.

LAGBAJA Anybody I know?

BANZA   Yes. Plenty of them. But nobody of value, if you must know. Swept away every house in

town except the beer-parlour. Killed everybody except, I suppose, you and me and
Sidi.

LAGBAJA   Nice woman, Sidi.

[*Reflective pause.*]

A woman like her I've never come across. Is
it true she used to clap very well?

BANZA   I've danced with her and seen her dance.

[*They dance.*]

A better dancer I'm yet to come across. But
I've never seen her clap.

LAGBAJA   One of these days I'm going to dance with
her.

BANZA   Sidi comes very expensive, I hope you know
that.

LAGBAJA   Money is not an object. I'll cut my balls and
mortgage them for Sidi.

BANZA   Then you'll be pretty useless to her, I'm
afraid.

LAGBAJA   Producing kids like a guinea-pig is no longer
the thing in vogue.

BANZA   Then commit suicide, my friend. De-congest
the human race.

LAGBAJA   I did try once. Jumped off the top of a
twenty-storey building.

BANZA   [*sceptically*] And what happened after that?

LAGBAJA   I woke up from the nightmare, sweating.

[*Pause.*]

It rained yesterday, did you know that?

BANZA   It's been so many years since it last rained.

LAGBAJA   Cats and dogs. Bolts of lightning like burning spears across the sky. Thunder ...

BANZA   And the ground?

LAGBAJA   Wet, so wet. And soft.

BANZA   Did it drop like pebbles?

LAGBAJA   And more. Like rocks rolling down a valley.

BANZA   And the farms? Did it fall on them and ease the thirst of their parched tongues?

LAGBAJA   They have no tongues.

BANZA   What?

LAGBAJA   The farms.

BANZA   But it fell on them, all the same?

LAGBAJA   All the same, it fell on them. The people rejoiced as well.

BANZA   The people are always rejoicing.

LAGBAJA   What's wrong with that?

BANZA   Sooner or later, they're back there crying again.

          [*He brings out the cigarette tin.*]

          Did I tell you I met God yesterday?

LAGBAJA   Can you spare one?

          [*He receives a cigarette from* BANZA, *who has stood up and headed for the door.*]

For three whole days I've been looking forward to this. A cigarette to smoke.

[*He sniffs the cigarette.* BANZA *goes out.*]

[*to the nearest member of the audience*] Three whole days, oh God, and here I am, the proud possessor of one.

[*The phone begins to ring. It should continue ringing until* BANZA *returns, bursting in through the door. He is drenched to the bone. The only dry object on him is the cigarette between his lips.*]

[*The phone stops ringing. Momentarily.*]

Gone for a swim?

[BANZA *is shivering. He brings out a box of wet matches and takes out one soaked matchstick after another, unsuccessfully trying to light the cigarette between his lips.*]

BANZA It's started again. The rain. Street outside is totally submerged. People are having to use canoes to cross.

LAGBAJA What do we do? Stay at home and lose our jobs?

BANZA No street to clean, man, the street's been swept away.

LAGBAJA Come on, let's get going.

[BANZA *is still rubbing one wet matchstick after another on the matchbox in his bid to light the cigarette.*]

BANZA   I said it's raining, didn't you hear me?

[LAGBAJA *is still sniffing his cigarette. He hands it back to* BANZA.]

[*The phone starts ringing again.* BANZA *eyes the phone, looking worried.*]

It could be Sidi.

LAGBAJA   [*ominously*] And then it could be not.

[*He begins to leave.*]

I shall see you when I come back. Don't forget to make supper.

[*He leaves through the door.*]

[*Sound of heavy rain.*]

[BANZA *eyes the phone, then eyes the door. He repeats this sequence of movements. He seems to panic.*]

BANZA   Hey you bastard, wait for me!

[*He runs after* LAGBAJA. *The phone continues to ring.*]

[*Slow fade to black.*]

END OF ACT ONE

ACT TWO: *Howling*

The lights come up on the room. Except for an old rusty pistol lying rather conspicuously on the table between BANZA *and* LAGBAJA, *it is as before.*

It is dead of night.

In the distance the barking and whining of a dog. The phlegmatic and abortive starting of an aged and consumptive car. A shrill protracted scream.

LAGBAJA   Did you hear that?

BANZA   [*irritably*] What? I didn't hear anything. Not a sound.

LAGBAJA   A dog barking.

BANZA   Dogs are meant to bark.

LAGBAJA   It was also whining.

BANZA   That too is in the nature of a dog.

LAGBAJA   In my village it's an evil omen. A dog only whines like that when death is lurking around the corner.

BANZA   Perhaps it's about to die

LAGBAJA   [*overlapping*] Perhaps it's about to die ... Did you hear the car?

BANZA   What car?

LAGBAJA   There was a car out there that was trying to start.

BANZA   Did it ... ?

LAGBAJA ... start? No, it didn't.

BANZA Even the key to success doesn't always fit into your ignition, no?

LAGBAJA Someone out there was screaming. And I could have sworn it was a woman.

BANZA Perhaps she was ...

LAGBAJA On second thoughts, I think it was a man.

BANZA ... being raped?

LAGBAJA Oh God! I hope it wasn't that.

BANZA But supposing it was? It is perfectly in the nature of men to rape women, and women to rape men, and women to rape women, and men to rape men ...

LAGBAJA ... sometimes they simply make love.

BANZA ... and sometimes it's hard to tell the difference.

[*Pause.*]

You saw the sign yourself: "You are requested not to throw cigarette ends in the urinals as it makes them soggy and damp, and difficult to light." [*pained*] You saw the sign.

[*Pause.*]

LAGBAJA Yes. There is evil out there, Temedu.

BANZA There is nothing out there. Nothing but this failure that is everywhere.

LAGBAJA There is evil out there, I tell you. Haven't we had this conversation before?

BANZA   Before you died, yes, a long, very long time
           ago.

           [LAGBAJA *looks at him strangely.*]

LAGBAJA   Before I died?

BANZA   You died. Don't you know that you died?

LAGBAJA   From one friend to another, I strongly sug-
           gest that you seek the help of a psychiatrist
           as a matter of the utmost urgency, my
           friend.

BANZA   But I killed you. I did kill you. Don't you
           remember that I killed you?

LAGBAJA   No doubt you've taken leave of your senses.

BANZA   But I tell you! You died. I killed you. You
           died and resurrected.

LAGBAJA   You're absolutely insane.

BANZA   I shot you in the head. With this — this!

           [LAGBAJA *takes the pistol and examines it,
           then tosses it back on the table.*]

LAGBAJA   You're certified. An intellectual eunuch. Ab-
           solutely hysterical. You should be commit-
           ted.

BANZA   [*astounded*] Are you denying that you died?
           That you resurrected?

LAGBAJA   Not only that. I'd add also that every word
           you utter detracts from the sum total of your
           sanity. You're psychoschizophrenic.

           [*Pause.*]

           Uuumh, that sounded nice. Nice. The more

my life falls apart, the more my vocabulary seems to improve.

[*Pause.*]

Have they set him free?

BANZA   Who?

LAGBAJA   Him.

BANZA   Him?

LAGBAJA   Him.

BANZA   Well, have they ... ?

LAGBAJA   ... set him free?

BANZA   No, they haven't.

LAGBAJA   They haven't?

BANZA   They haven't.

LAGBAJA   Then they must have killed him.

BANZA   Tortured him to death, yes. I worked there once, remember? The Department of Persuasion. We used to cut out their balls. Squeeze them out. Orange pips.

LAGBAJA   He couldn't be ...

BANZA   ... dead?

LAGBAJA   But he must be.

BANZA   But he must be.

LAGBAJA   You think he might be dead?

BANZA   I think he's dead. Hung for a heretic.

LAGBAJA   Then he must surely be dead.

BANZA   He definitely is dead.

[*Pause.*]

Not that I would exactly mourn him.

LAGBAJA You wouldn't?

BANZA I once caught him with my wife, the bastard.

LAGBAJA You once caught him with your wife?

BANZA Talking to her. The bastard. Talking to my wife.

[*Pause.*]

LAGBAJA I have an erection.

BANZA Sorry, I'm a married man.

[LAGBAJA *stands up. He fiddles with his zipper and makes as if to masturbate.*]

LAGBAJA May I?

BANZA [*starts furiously*] Did I hear you right? Say that again!

LAGBAJA I said, may I ... ?

BANZA [*further enraged*] Every sperm is special.
Do you hear that?
Every sperm is great.
If one sperm is wasted,
God gets quite irate.

[*Pause.*]

Have you never seen that graffito? Don't you ever read?

LAGBAJA [*genuinely contrite*] Oh, I'm sorry, very sorry. I didn't know that. I've never seen any graffito. I didn't know that. Honest to God, I didn't.

BANZA   Didn't know what?

LAGBAJA   That God was capable of emotions.

           [*Pause.*]

           I still have a hard-on.

BANZA   So go to town, man! Paint the town red! Get
           yourself a pumpkin.

           [*Pause.*]

LAGBAJA   I prefer a woman.

BANZA   There you go again, sniffing a gift horse in
           the mouth.

LAGBAJA   And where does he stand in this matter?

BANZA   Who?

LAGBAJA   God. Won't he get irate?

BANZA   Probably sulk for a day or two. Then he'll go
           minding his own business.

LAGBAJA   Give your life to him, man! Give your life to
           him!

BANZA   And if I do give my life to him, what will I be
           left with?

LAGBAJA   But he saves, you know, he saves.

BANZA   And why can't we also? We'll make it a joint
           account.

           [*Pause.*]

           Have you never seen a corpse smiling?

LAGBAJA   [*uneasily*] No, I haven't.

BANZA   Sometimes, you know, sometimes I'm over-
           come with a paranoia: I'm the last human

being left on earth and I'm surrounded by five billion corpses. Phew! Five billion. The thought makes me grin like a fool.

[*Pause.*]

Do you know that a man's beard continues to grow even after he's dead? And the nails as well. Until you begin to rot. I was once a morgue attendant, you know. Before the flood. Superb job. Made you feel like God. Sometimes after yet another of those multiple accidents involving those luxury buses, and the casualties were brought in and stacked one upon the other like so many lumps of yam in a barn, I'd stand among them, these denizens of the graves, alone, savouring the gut-smell of blood and bile and decay that filled the air like sour-sweet mango perfume. I would stand among them, smiling back at those who smiled ... [*demonstrates*] "Hello, baby, how're you doing? I like the way you smile. Like a bloody bitch. I like the way you smile. Honest to God I do. Like the patron saint of all bitches. If there's a hell, I'll meet you there. Buy you a drink. And that's a date."

[*Pause.*]

"Hello, old man." [*fondles an imaginary protrusion*] "Now, that's my man. Went and croaked with a hard-on, didn't we? I've got half a mind to give you a blow-job right now. Just to see the look on God's face. I bet you must have been some teenage idiot's sugar daddy. Were you thinking dirty when it happened? A big problem for the undertaker, I hope you realise that, you fool. Dying with an erection, for God's sakes, have you no decency?" [*to* LAGBAJA] The more I look at you, the more I'm reminded of those corpses. You look — ordinary — most inordinately ordinary, have I never told you? Every time I look at your face I have this nauseating feeling that you could have been anyone else. You could have been me, for instance. Or my father or even my mother. You could have been anybody. Anybody. But ... [*spits in disgust*] ... you chose to be you. I could sometimes almost mistake you for myself when we meet in the doorway.

> [*He turns pointedly towards* LAGBAJA, *who has all this while been staring passively into space, a fatuous grin permanently installed on his face.*]

Have we never met in the doorway? [*waits in vain for a response*] I suppose we must have. Or you wouldn't have that smug look in your eyes. You could choke a man to death with the stench of that smugness.

> [*He stares furiously at* LAGBAJA's *passive, almost idiotic, absolutely smugness-bereft presence.*]

You are the smuggest bastard I've ever met, do you hear, do you ...

> [*Pause.*]

Time is passing.

[*Pause.*]

I wonder what else it should be doing. Every minute of my life I've been the sole witness to the birth of another minute. It's the most monotonous experience you could witness. God is a rather dodgy old sod, is what I say. I wish he would do something distantly radical one of these days. Stop the hand of the clock, for instance. But I guess he couldn't. Might give him an orgasm, stain the holy robe, you see. And that'd mean a police record. Ruin his chances of a re-election.

LAGBAJA [*the vacant look still on his face*] Why did you kill her?

BANZA Who?

LAGBAJA Why did you kill her?

BANZA *Who?*

LAGBAJA I said why ...

BANZA [*overlapping*] I was framed.

LAGBAJA Oh.

[*Pause.*]

[*with a look — hesitant at first — of distress at his groin, slowly*] I — I think I ought to tell you something, Temedu.

BANZA [*sighs*] There are so many things in this life you ought to tell me.

LAGBAJA It's four days gone now, Temedu, and I still haven't had my period.

[*In the distance the barking and whining of
a dog. The phlegmatic and abortive starting of an aged and consumptive car. A
shrill protracted scream.*]

Did you hear that?

BANZA [*irritably*] What? I didn't hear anything. Not
a sound.

LAGBAJA A dog barking.

BANZA Dogs are meant to bark.

LAGBAJA It was also whining.

BANZA That too is in the nature of a dog.

LAGBAJA In my village it's an evil omen. A dog only
whines like that when death is lurking
around the corner.

BANZA Perhaps it's about to die.

LAGBAJA [*overlapping*] Perhaps it's about to die ... Did
you hear the car?

BANZA What car?

LAGBAJA There was a car out there that was trying to
start.

BANZA Did it ... ?

LAGBAJA ... start? No, it didn't.

BANZA Even the key to success doesn't always fit
into your ignition, no?

LAGBAJA Someone out there was screaming. And I
could have sworn it was a woman.

BANZA Perhaps she was ...

LAGBAJA   On second thoughts, I think it was a man.

BANZA   ... being raped?

[*Pause.*]

LAGBAJA   Did you see the lights?

BANZA   What lights?

LAGBAJA   At the end of the tunnel.

BANZA   A train approaching, perhaps?

[*Pause.*]

LAGBAJA   Perhaps. There is evil out there, Temedu.

BANZA   There is nothing out there. Nothing but this failure that is everywhere.

LAGBAJA   There is evil out there, I tell you.

BANZA   [*in exasperation*] Very well then. There is evil out there. Shall we go looking for it with a handgun?

LAGBAJA   [*dejectedly*] Perhaps after all that's what we should do. Get ourselves some handguns.

BANZA   We will, we will. We'll line the whole lot of them evil-doers out there, we'll line them up at a seaside stadium with their backs to the sea and their faces to the sand. And shoot them. Every last one of them. We'll shoot them. Spill out their evil-churning guts and declare surplus for the vultures. [*facing* LAGBAJA] Isn't that what we should do? We'll do it, don't you worry. So long as you don't come crying to me when you see them resurrecting three days later. A certain Jewish gentleman did that two thousand years ago if you remember and ever since it's become something of a fashion.

LAGBAJA I'd like to see them do that. Resurrect. Really I would. You have a saying, don't you? The one about trespassers.

BANZA Which one?

[*Pause.*]

You keep intruding on my thoughts. Every time I come up with a lofty idea you spirit it out with your endless chatter. If I had my way I would've shot you ages ago.

LAGBAJA And supposing I survived?

BANZA I'd shoot you again.

LAGBAJA Naturally. Don't you think that's what we should do to them out there?

BANZA What? Shoot them down every time they come up for air?

LAGBAJA Shoot them down every time they come up for air.

BANZA By the time we're finished we'll probably be right there beside them — clawing out for a reed to hang on to.

[*Pause.*]

LAGBAJA [*hesitantly*] Excuse me.

BANZA [*impatiently*] Yes?

LAGBAJA May I wank off?

[*He turns his back on* BANZA *and proceeds to masturbate.*]

BANZA   It's someone's birthday today — yours or mine. I cannot remember the last time I had a birthday. Birthdays are for howling, I always say, for letting go. Go to the highest point you can find and howl to him up there: "Pull back the time, you cheat! You keep it all and only dole it out in trickles to us. Give us back all those centuries you've stolen from us! And what makes you think we don't know why you queue us up and kill us so? Because it's the only way you can go on being alive." I swear to you, Temedu, the day we find the key to immortality, God will simply drop dead.

[*Pause.*]

What did you say?

[LAGBAJA *is not in a state to say anything. He is masturbating.*]

That he'll kill us all before we can? Well, I've got news for you: he can't kill us.

LAGBAJA [*as he climaxes*] He can't? Who can't?

BANZA   God. Because if he does, he'll have destroyed himself as well.

LAGBAJA How?

BANZA   He wouldn't exist if there wasn't you and me to think that he does.

LAGBAJA No?

BANZA   No. The boss is only boss for as long as he has someone to boss over.

LAGBAJA   I feel — good.

[*He brings out a wine glass from behind him. It is filled to the brim with a thick, milky substance.*]

BANZA   What's that?

[*He takes it from* LAGBAJA *and takes a sip.*]

Tastes like come.

LAGBAJA   Semi-skimmed. There was that case of the celibate monk some time ago who started secreting a milky substance from his sweat glands. Turned out to be sperm.

[*Pause.*]

If you'd pricked my skin with a needle five minutes ago that's what would have come oozing out, not blood. I was full to bursting point.

BANZA   Have we not had this conversation before?

LAGBAJA   Not with you I haven't.

BANZA   I seem to remember it from another life a long time ago. I could have sworn that I was here a thousand years ago, this very minute a thousand years ago, sitting at this very spot, on another seat very much like this one and with another fool who could well have been you. [*looks at himself dejectedly.*] Only thing is, I don't seem to have changed at all.

LAGBAJA   But you have. But you have.

BANZA   Really? You think so?

LAGBAJA   I know so. I should, shouldn't I?

[*Pause.*]

I'm your father after all.

BANZA   [*betraying no surprise whatever*] You are my father?

LAGBAJA   To the last pint of blood, yes. To the nearest genetic hundred. I gave you birth, don't you remember?

BANZA   But how could I?

LAGBAJA   You were the fastest growing kid I've ever known — started walking at age six months and turned to crawling three months later. You crawled for fifteen years to a day.

BANZA   [*beaming with pride*] I did? I've always known it too. I knew there was something — something special about me. [*becoming more friendly*] So you're my father?

[*He extends his hand for a shake. The hand hangs awkwardly in the air for some time then drops. Immediately it drops, LAGBAJA extends his own hand, also for a shake, and is similarly rebuffed. LAGBAJA's hand drops. They are both grinning from ear to ear.*]

So you are my father.

LAGBAJA   Yes I am.

BANZA   So you are my father.

LAGBAJA   Yes I am.

BANZA   So you are my father.

LAGBAJA   Yes I am.

> [BANZA *erupts in happy laughter while* LAGBAJA *looks on with a deathly grimace. The moment* BANZA *stops laughing,* LAGBAJA *bursts into his own convulsive laughter while* BANZA *looks on with a puzzled grimace.*]

BANZA   [*totally expressionless*] This must be the happiest day of my life.

LAGBAJA   [*yawns*] Mine too.

> [*Pause.*]

BANZA   [*sudden change of mood*] Do you know what I think of you? What I really think of you?

LAGBAJA   [*cowering*] No. What do you think of me?

BANZA   [*relaxes*] You are a good fellow. Beneath contempt, but a nice kind of person. I would kill you. And I will too. Such a pity. We could have visited with each other till we were both old.

LAGBAJA   [*yawns*] Yeah, such a poor pity. But you have no choice, have you? You will kill me.

BANZA   Unfortunately, yes. I've got no choice. I just have to.

LAGBAJA   Such a pity too. Poor fellow. I wish I could help, honest to God, I wish I could. But —

[*He gestures helplessly.*]

BANZA   Don't you sometimes wish you were dead?

LAGBAJA   There are so many things I wish I were. But if horses were wishes ...

BANZA   And don't you sometimes wish you'd wake up after three days?

LAGBAJA   That's called a coma.

BANZA   Did I tell you about my father — how he died?

[LAGBAJA *nods.*]

I was eight years old then, or five or twenty, or five and twenty. We were on a country-wide tour, my father and I. He had this car then, a blue station-wagon. The make is irrelevant. The place insignificant. We were on this long lonesome highway, I remember, and my father, being the reckless driver he was, was making a steady twenty miles an hour. Really taking his time, you'll agree with me, considering that the car couldn't go any faster, simply taking his time. We had the road to ourselves for close to two hours when, suddenly, from behind us came this big monster of a truck. One moment he was behind us, the next it was dead level with us. We wouldn't really have noticed the bastard if he'd simply sped past us and left us in our shells. But no way; for the next half hour the idiot simply remained level with us, and of course this began to irritate my father. I mean, a man can only take so much ... Father leaned out of the car and screamed: "Move, you bushman!" Or that was what I thought he was going to say, because that was everybody's middle name as far as my father was concerned — bushman. But he never got to saying anything: the moment his head came leaning out of the car, I saw this short devil of an axe come slashing down on his neck from the truck. The axe went right through, neatly severing the head from the body. A perfect work of art. I nearly wept, seeing my father's head that day, rolling on the highway like a stray ball. But father was a man of firm resolutions. He was. Didn't utter another word until thirty minutes later — when he brought out his handkerchief to wipe the sweat off his face and that was when, for the first time, he noticed that he hadn't got a head. And burst into tears.

[*Pause.*]

That was the only time I ever saw him cry.

LAGBAJA   Sad story. A bloody sad story. A sad and bloody story. I'll remember it any other time I feel like a bad mood.

[*Pause.*]

Temedu.

BANZA   Yes, Temedu.

LAGBAJA   I have an erection.

BANZA   You have an erection?

LAGBAJA   I have an erection.

BANZA   You have an erection?

LAGBAJA   I wish I could set him free.

BANZA   Who?

LAGBAJA   Him.

BANZA   Him?

LAGBAJA   Him.

BANZA   He called God a common thief.

LAGBAJA   No, it wasn't God he called a thief. It was one of his prophets.

BANZA   Same thing. If you ask me.

LAGBAJA   Tell me, why do these gods always turn out to be false?

           [BANZA *picks up the pistol and begins to load it.*]

BANZA   I've never known one to be a god.

LAGBAJA   This one thinks he creates. Creates.

BANZA   But he does, doesn't he? And then destroys. One comes after the other, not so? Like marriage and divorce.

LAGBAJA   Mere masturbation, if you ask me.

BANZA   Sheer wastage. Totally useless. All the same, I sometimes wish they'd set him free.

LAGBAJA   God? They jailed God?

BANZA   No. Him.

LAGBAJA   But you know his crime. You're aware of its enormity.

BANZA   He said we were even more irresponsible than God. He said that. He compared us with God.

LAGBAJA   He did?

BANZA   He did. And worse.

LAGBAJA   In that case, in the light of this additional evidence, I hope he rots in jail.

BANZA   I hope he rots in jail.

> [*Pause.*]

> [*politely*] Please let me know when you're ready.

LAGBAJA   Ready for what?

> [BANZA *waves the pistol apologetically in the air.*]

BANZA   There's only one bullet left ...

LAGBAJA   [*sarcastically*] ... and it's got my name written on it? Is that what you're trying to say?

BANZA   [*quiet desperation*] I can't afford to miss.

LAGBAJA   Not to worry. You just aim for my head.

> [*He stands up and extends his hand for a shake.* BANZA *ignores it.* LAGBAJA's *hand hangs awkwardly in the air for a while then drops. Immediately it drops,* BANZA *extends his own hand, also for a shake and is in turn rebuffed.* BANZA's *hand drops. They are both grinning from ear to ear.*]

Thanks for everything, my man. I'll miss you.

BANZA   I'll miss you too, father.

LAGBAJA   Is my bag packed?

BANZA   Everything.

LAGBAJA   My whisky case. If you should forget to pack my whisky case, I'll die of thirst over there. I hope you know that.

BANZA   Rest assured, father, I personally packed it myself.

LAGBAJA   And my carton of cigarettes?

BANZA   You don't smoke.

LAGBAJA   And I'm a vegetarian, and I drink decaffeinated coffee. Did you or did you not pack my carton of cigarettes, boy?

BANZA   [*quietly*] Everything is packed.

LAGBAJA   Are you ... ?

BANZA   I said, everything is packed, father. Trust me.

LAGBAJA   [*musingly*] In the old days, when the king died he was accompanied by his chief Horseman. You're lucky these days if you go with a carton of cigarettes. What has the world come to?

[BANZA *aims the pistol carefully at* LAGBAJA's *head.*]

BANZA   Goodbye, father. Say me well to mother.

LAGBAJA   [*pained*] What has the world come to?

[BANZA *pulls the trigger. It merely clicks. There is no bullet in the pistol.*]

BANZA   [*as* LAGBAJA *comes crashing against the bar*]
         And don't you forget to resurrect!

> [LAGBAJA *falls down as if lifeless.* BANZA
> *turns slowly round, a look of fear, of terror,
> slowly creeping onto his face. He gingerly
> drops the pistol on the table — and begins
> to go off. At first he walks slowly, then he
> makes as if to break into a race. He freezes
> in that position.*]

> [*Blackout.*]

> [*In the distance the barking and whining of
> a dog. The phlegmatic and abortive start-
> ing of an aged and consumptive car. A
> shrill protracted scream. As* BANZA *comes
> running back on stage, there is a new and
> deeper terror now on his face.*]

> [*Lights up.*]

> [LAGBAJA *is seated by the table, an idiotic
> grin stuck like plaster on his face.*]

LAGBAJA   Did you hear that?

BANZA   [*irritably*] What? I didn't hear anything. Not
          a sound.

LAGBAJA   A dog barking.

BANZA   Dogs are meant to bark.

LAGBAJA   It was also whining.

BANZA   That too is in the nature of a dog.

LAGBAJA   In my village it's an evil omen. A dog only
          whines like that when death is lurking
          around the corner.

BANZA   Perhaps it's about to die.

LAGBAJA [*overlapping*] Perhaps it's about to die ... Did you hear the car?

BANZA   What car?

LAGBAJA There was a car out there that was trying to start.

BANZA   Did it ... ?

LAGBAJA ... start? No it didn't.

BANZA   Even the key to success doesn't always fit into your ignition, no?

LAGBAJA Someone out there was screaming. And I could have sworn it was a woman.

BANZA   Perhaps she was ...

LAGBAJA On second thoughts, I think it was a man.

BANZA   ... being raped.

         [*Pause.*]

LAGBAJA Did you see the light?

BANZA   What light?

LAGBAJA At the end of the tunnel.

BANZA   There was a light at the end of the tunnel?

LAGBAJA Yes.

BANZA   Are you sure?

LAGBAJA Yes.

BANZA   In that case, I don't think it matters whether or not I saw it.

         [*Pause.*]

[*He takes out from his pocket a tin ciga-rette case. He brings out cigarette after cigarette. They are all soaking wet.*]

[*angrily, to* LAGBAJA] You saw the sign your-self: "You are requested not to throw cigar-ette ends in the urinals as it makes them soggy and damp, and difficult to light." You saw the sign, and yet ...   [*to himself*] I should've laid them out to dry.

LAGBAJA   There is evil out there, Temedu.

BANZA   There is nothing out there. Nothing but this failure that is everywhere. [*looking at the cigarettes sadly*] I should've laid them out to dry.

LAGBAJA   There is evil out there, I tell you. Haven't we had this conversation before?

BANZA   [*to himself*] I should've ... [*He seems to snap out of it.*] ... what? ... Before you died, yes, a long, a very long time ago.

[LAGBAJA *looks at him strangely.*]

LAGBAJA   What's that supposed to mean — before I died?

BANZA   You died. Don't you know that you died?

LAGBAJA   From one friend to another, I strongly sug-gest that you seek the help of a psychiatrist as a matter of the utmost urgency, my friend.

BANZA   But I killed you. I did kill you. Don't you remember that I killed you?

LAGBAJA   No doubt you've taken leave of your senses.

BANZA   But I tell you! You died. I killed you. You died and resurrected.

LAGBAJA   You're absolutely insane.

BANZA   I shot you in the head! With this — this.

    [LAGBAJA *takes the pistol and examines it, then tosses it back on the table.*]

LAGBAJA   You're certified. An intellectual eunuch. Absolutely hysterical. You should be committed.

BANZA   Are you denying that you died? That you resurrected?

LAGBAJA   Not only that. I'd add also that every word you utter detracts from the sum total of your sanity. You're psychoschizophrenic.

    [*Pause.*]

    Uuumh, that sounded nice. Nice.

    [*Pause.*]

    Have they set him free?

BANZA   Your father?

LAGBAJA   [*overlapping*] My—

BANZA   I'm your father. I'm free. On parole, at least.

LAGBAJA   You're my—?

BANZA   [*overlapping*] I'm your father. To the last pint of blood. To the nearest genetic hundred. You want proof? You were pregnant once — remember? Remember the abortion? I was that abortionist.

LAGBAJA   But you're dead. Aren't you dead? Your head was cut off. The baby sued, remember? She took exception to being aborted.

BANZA   [*hotly protesting*] It was nothing personal ...

LAGBAJA   You were found guilty ...

BANZA   A frame-up ... it was a frame-up ...

LAGBAJA   ... and convicted. You were beheaded.

BANZA   Spare Parts. I walked into the Spare Parts department one evening when no-one was watching and picked up another one.

LAGBAJA   Bullshit.

[*Pause.*]

It rained yesterday.

BANZA   It did?

LAGBAJA   The ground was wet.

BANZA   And that's news? That strikes you as unusual?

LAGBAJA   People brought out their umbrellas.

BANZA   Now that's unusual. Usually they simply dash through the rain and hope for the best. And those without umbrellas?

LAGBAJA   Raincoats. Mackintoshes.

BANZA   The only argument against a raging downpour is to put on a raincoat. They put on raincoats. That's — wise. And those without raincoats, mackintoshes?

LAGJABA   Got beaten by the rain, of course.

BANZA   And why should some have umbrellas and others none?

LAGBAJA   I'd like you to tell me. It's always been like that.

BANZA   Always?

LAGBAJA   Always.

BANZA   Are the horses ready?

[*Pause.*]

LAGBAJA   What horses?

BANZA   I thought — I thought... I thought we were...

LAGBAJA   Horsemen?

BANZA   I thought we were horsemen.

LAGBAJA   Yes.

BANZA   There were four of us.

LAGBAJA   Yes.

BANZA   [*insistently*] There were four of us!

LAGBAJA   Yes.

BANZA   What happened ... ?

LAGBAJA   To ...

BANZA   Yes ...

LAGBAJA   The flood did for them. They drowned.

BANZA   They drowned?

LAGBAJA   Yes. But we survived.

BANZA   They drowned. We survived.

LAGBAJA   Yes. We survived.

BANZA   We're survivors.

LAGBAJA   Yes.

BANZA   We survived.

LAGBAJA   Yes.

BANZA   We'll always survive.

LAGBAJA   Yes.

BANZA   There'll be bad times and not-so-good times.
           Good times and so-so times. But we'll always
           survive.

LAGBAJA   [*happily, like a prayer*] Yes, yes, yes, yes. Oh
           God, yes. [*Pause.*] This must be the happiest
           day of my life.

BANZA   Mine too.

           [LAGBAJA *erupts in happy laughter while*
           BANZA *looks on with a deathly grimace.*
           The moment LAGBAJA *stops laughing,*
           BANZA *bursts into his own convulsive*
           laughter while LAGBAJA *looks on with a*
           puzzled grimace.]

           [*Instant black.*]

           THE END

By the same author

MARCHING FOR FAUSA

MARCHING FOR FAUSA is set in Songi, capital city of the Federal Republic of Songhai, a populous country on the west coast of Africa. A young journalist and photographer, Telene Balarabe, is investigating the disappearance of a group of schoolchildren who have been arrested by the State Security Service during a public demonstration.

"[*Marching for Fausa*] simply crackles with anger and dark laughter. It's as if Dario Fo had written a fiery and ferocious political parable."   *John Peter, Sunday Times*

"A powerful play about the evils of dictatorship."
     Michael Billington, Guardian

For a free copy of our list of plays and theatre books write to:
Amber Lane Press, Church Street, Charlbury, Oxford OX7 3PR
Telephone and fax: 0608 810024